CRABTREE CONTACT

DESERT SURVIVAL GUIDE

Ben Hubbard

Skull, Namibia

🌴 Crabtree Publishing Company

www.crabtreebooks.com

Crabtree Publishing Company

www.crabtreebooks.com

1-800-387-7650

PMB 59051
350 Fifth Avenue, 59th Floor
New York, NY, 10118

616 Welland Avenue,
St. Catharines, Ontario
L2M 5V6

Content development by
Shakespeare Squared

Published by
Crabtree Publishing
Company © 2010

www.ShakespeareSquared.com

First published
in Great Britain in
2010 by TickTock
Entertainment Ltd.

Printed in the
U.S.A./122009
CG20091120

Crabtree Publishing
Company credits:
Project manager: Kathy Middleton
Editor: Reagan Miller
Proofreader: Crystal Sikkens
Production coordinator: Katherine Berti
Prepress technician: Katherine Berti

TickTock credits:
Publisher: Melissa Fairley
Art director: Faith Booker
Editor: Emma Dods
Designer: Emma Randall
Production controller: Ed Green
Production manager: Suzy Kelly

Thank you to Lorraine Petersen and the members of nasen

Picture credits (t=top; b=bottom; c=centre; l=left; r=right; OFC=outside front cover;): John
Cancalosi/ardea.com: 13t. Michael Freeman/Corbis: 7. George Grall/Getty Images: 24.
imagebroker/Alamy: 28–29. Mauritius/SuperStock: 26. Shutterstock: 1, 2, 4, 5, 6 (both),
8 (both), 9t, 10, 11 (both), 12t, 16 (all), 17 (both), 18–19 (all), 20–21 (all), 22–23, 25, 27
(both), 29t (both), 31C, 31D. Karl Terblanche/ardea.com: 12b. Anne-Marie Weber/Corbis:
9b, 31A. Woods Wheatcroft/Getty Images: 14, 31B. Gordon Wiltsie/Getty Images: 13b.
www.janespencer.com: 15. iStock: OFCc, OBCb. Shutterstock: OFCbl, OFCt, OBCt.

Every effort has been made to trace copyright holders, and we apologize in advance
for any omissions. We would be pleased to insert the appropriate acknowledgments
in any subsequent edition of this publication.

Library and Archives Canada Cataloguing in Publication

Owen, Ruth, 1967-
        Desert survival guide / Ruth Owen.

(Crabtree contact)
Includes index.
ISBN 978-0-7787-7532-4 (bound).--ISBN 978-0-7787-7554-6 (pbk.)

                1. Desert survival--Juvenile literature. I. Title.
III. Series: Crabtree contact

GV200.5.O94 2010   j613.6'909154   C2009-906790-0

Library of Congress Cataloging-in-Publication Data

Owen, Ruth, 1967-
  Desert survival guide / Ruth Owen.
        p. cm. -- (Crabtree contact)
  Includes index.
  ISBN 978-0-7787-7554-6 (pbk. : alk. paper)
  -- ISBN 978-0-7787-7532-4 (reinforced library binding : alk. paper)
  1. Desert survival--Juvenile literature. I. Title. II. Series.

GV200.5.O93 2010
613.6'9--dc22

2009047089

*Sahara Desert,
North Africa*

CONTENTS

CHAPTER 1 : LOST IN THE DESERT

In your everyday life you have everything you need to survive.

Turn on a tap and water pours out.
Pick up the phone and a pizza is on its way!

But what would happen if one day all that changed?

What would happen if you were driving across a **desert** and your car broke down?

Would you know how to survive in a desert?

A desert can be rocky with deep canyons.

canyon

A desert can also have huge sand dunes.

dune

There are often sandstorms in sandy deserts.

sandstorm

How to survive a sandstorm:
- If you cannot get to shelter, lie or sit down.
- Close your eyes or put on glasses.
- Cover your nose and mouth with some cloth.
- Point your body in the direction you were walking.

After the storm, everything will be covered in sand.
Everything will look different and you might get lost.

In a desert, everything looks the same. Look out for **landmarks**, such as a bush or large rock.

landmark

In the dry desert air, things can seem closer than they actually are. Always multiply your estimated distance by three—that is a desert survival trick!

If you are in a broken-down car, stay at the site if you can.

You may have to leave the site to find water and food. If this happens, use rocks or other materials to make a large arrow to show rescuers which direction you took.

rescue dog

REMEMBER
Find water, shelter, and food—in that order!

CHAPTER 2

FINDING WATER

In a hot desert, lack of water is your biggest enemy!

Your body cools off by sweating. The more you sweat, the more water your body loses.

If your body does not have enough water to sweat, you will get **heatstroke**. Heatstroke will make you pass out.

Find shade.

Do most of your walking at night when it is cool.

Do not take off your clothes. Cover your head and neck, too. Your clothes will soak up your sweat. The wet clothes will keep your body cool.

In a hot desert, your body needs 33.8 ounces (one liter) of water every hour. Sip water as often as you can.

Your **urine** should be pale yellow. If your urine is dark yellow, you are not getting enough water.

You need to find water as soon as possible.

storm clouds gather

Keep watch for storm clouds. Use anything you have to catch rainwater.

dune ant

Look for ants. A long line of ants on a tree could be a sign there is water trapped inside the tree.

Birds and other animals need water, too. Look for bird droppings on rocks. There might be water in a rock crack nearby.

Gambel's quail

If you find a dried-up stream, dig a hole in the ground. There could be water underground.

dried-up stream

CHAPTER 3

SHELTER

If you do not already have a shelter, you will need to find or build one. In a desert, the daytime temperature can reach 140°F (60°C).

Look around you. Caves, trees, and large bushes can provide shelter. The shelter will give you shade. This will keep you cool during the day. It will help your body to use less water.

cave

If you have a blanket or sheet of plastic you can build an underground shelter.

Find a low spot in the ground or dig a **trench**.

Stretch the blanket or plastic across the hole.

Pile up sand and rocks to hold the sheet in place.

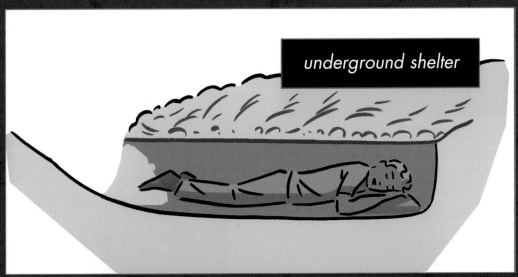

underground shelter

CHAPTER 4

FIRE

If you can find material to burn, build a fire. A fire can be used for cooking and will keep you warm at night.

To build a fire you need tinder, kindling, and fuel.

Tinder is material that will catch fire easily.

Use dry grass for tinder.

Then add kindling to help the fire burn strongly.

Use dry leaves or small twigs for kindling.

Use dry wood or branches for fuel.

Finally, you add fuel to make the fire burn for a long time.

If you do not have matches, you need to improvise. This means finding a new way to do something. A lens from glasses or a camera will catch sunlight. Use the lens to direct light from the Sun onto the tinder. Eventually, the tinder will get hot and catch fire.

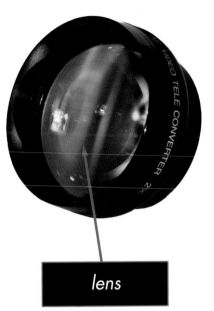

lens

CHAPTER 5

FINDING FOOD

In a desert, it is more important to find water than food. A healthy person can last about 40 days without food.

Your body uses up water digesting your food. So, if you only have a little water, do not eat.

You can eat insects such as ants, **termites**, beetles, and grasshoppers. You can also eat insect **larvae**.

ants

beetle

termite hill

grasshopper

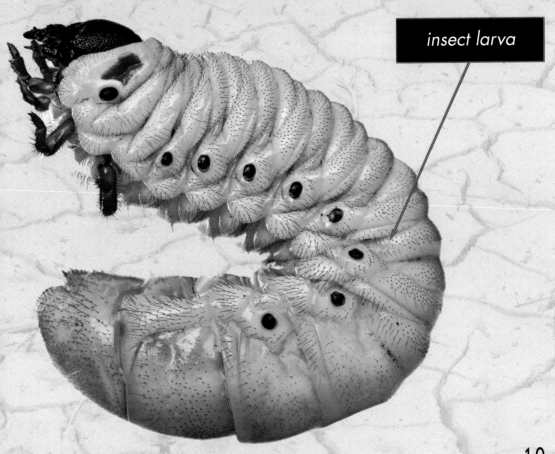

insect larva

19

The baobab tree grows in deserts in Africa and Australia. You can boil young baobab leaves in water to make soup.

You can also eat the tree's fruits. Break open the fruit and eat the soft **pulp** and seeds inside.

seeds and pulp inside
a baobab fruit

baobab tree

You can also eat the roots of a young baobab tree.

There are many snakes in the desert. Most snakes do not attack unless they are threatened. Keeping your distance is the best plan. But you might have to kill a snake to protect yourself.

Do not waste the meat! The snake's **venom** is behind its head. So, cut the snake in half. Then cook and eat the tail end.

spitting cobra

If you do not have a knife, you need to look for an animal skeleton. A sharp piece of bone can be used as a knife.

CHAPTER 6

DESERT DANGERS

In the desert, there are many creatures that can bite or sting.

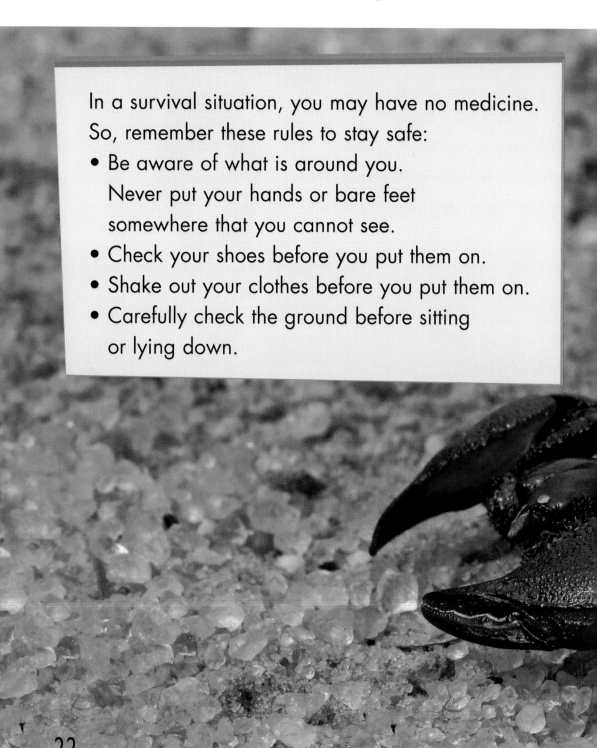

In a survival situation, you may have no medicine.
So, remember these rules to stay safe:

- Be aware of what is around you.
  Never put your hands or bare feet
  somewhere that you cannot see.
- Check your shoes before you put them on.
- Shake out your clothes before you put them on.
- Carefully check the ground before sitting
  or lying down.

Scorpions are relatives
of spiders. They have
a venomous stinger
on their tail.

scorpion in the desert

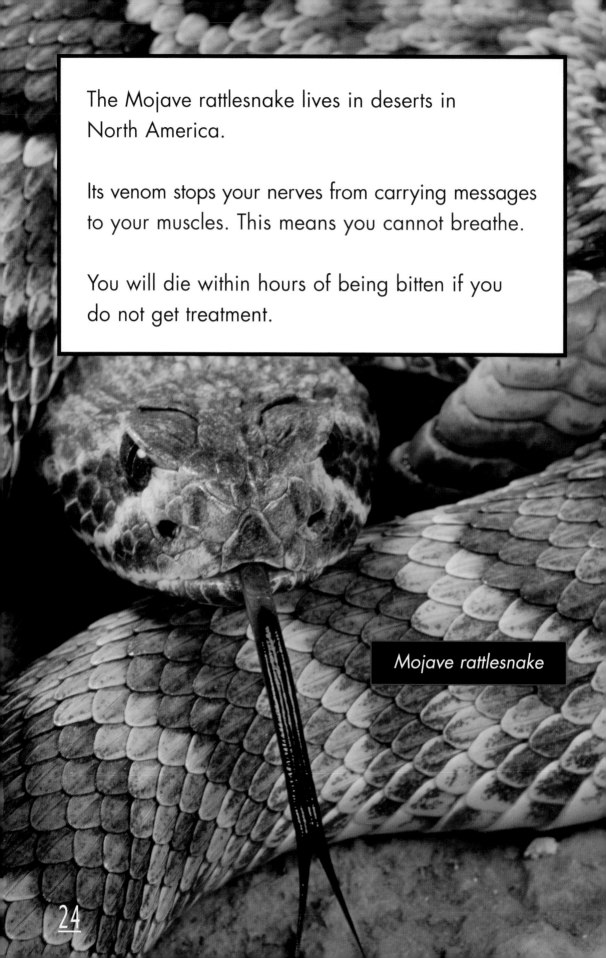

The Mojave rattlesnake lives in deserts in North America.

Its venom stops your nerves from carrying messages to your muscles. This means you cannot breathe.

You will die within hours of being bitten if you do not get treatment.

Mojave rattlesnake

The Gila monster lives in deserts in the U.S. and Mexico.

It is a type of lizard and can grow up to 19.7 inches (50 centimeters) long.

Gila monster

If you get too close, the Gila monster might bite. It uses its sharp teeth to hold on tight. Venom from its lower jaw will enter the wound.

CHAPTER 7

PROTECT YOUR BODY

You must keep your body clean in a survival situation. Dirty skin can become infected and cause illness.

If you do not have much water, take an "air bath."

Take off all your clothes before the day gets hot. Shake out your clothes to remove any loose dirt. Expose your body to the air for one hour.

Arak tree

In ancient times, people in the desert used twigs to clean their teeth. The twigs came from the Arak tree.

If you get sunburn, find an aloe vera plant. Cut open a leaf. Spread the plant's juice on your sunburn. The plant's juice will help relieve the pain of the sunburn.

leaf

aloe vera

aloe vera juice

CHAPTER 8

RESCUE

You need to make sure a rescue plane can see you.

Making a fire is a good way to get noticed.

You can send a message to a rescue plane, too. Use rocks to make the signs shown below. Pilots around the world know what these signs mean. The signs should be as large as possible so pilots can spot them from high up in the air.

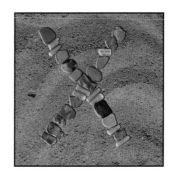

V means "help is needed."
X means "medical help is needed."
If a plane sees your signs, it will tilt its wings from side to side to let you know help is on the way.

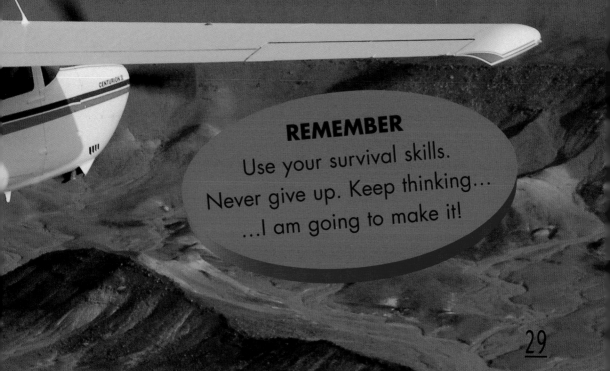

REMEMBER
Use your survival skills.
Never give up. Keep thinking…
…I am going to make it!

NEED-TO-KNOW WORDS

canyon A valley with steep, cliff-like walls. A canyon is cut into Earth by flowing water. A canyon can take thousands or millions of years to form

desert A dry area where less than ten inches (25 centimeters) of rain falls each year

dune A hill made from sand. A dune forms when wind blows large quantities of sand into a pile that gets bigger and bigger

heatstroke A condition that can happen when the body gets too hot and cannot cool itself. A person with heatstroke will feel ill and dizzy. They may pass out. If the condition gets worse, it can harm the brain, liver, kidneys, and other parts of the body

landmark Something that a person can use to figure out where they are

larvae The young of many insects, including ants and termites. Larvae hatch from eggs

pulp The soft part of a fruit inside the skin or shell

termites Small insects that look similar to ants. Termites live in large colonies

trench A carved out ditch in the ground

urine Liquid waste released when emptying the bladder

venom A poison that is deliberately passed onto a victim through a bite or sting

SURVIVAL PATTERNS

In a survival situation, you must form a survival pattern. The pattern will put your daily tasks into order—the most important tasks first. You must stick to your pattern each day. Here are the things that will be included in a desert survival pattern:

water

shelter

fire

food

SURVIVAL ONLINE

Learn more desert survival tips.
www.discoverychannel.co.uk/survival_zone/environments/ desert/index.shtml

Discover facts and pictures of desert life around the world.
http://environment.nationalgeographic.com/environment/ habitats/desert-profile.html

Find out how to build a special pit for collecting water, called a "still."
www.desertusa.com/mag98/dec/stories/water.html

Publisher's note to educators and parents:
Our editors have carefully reviewed these Web sites to ensure that they are suitable for children. Many Web sites change frequently, however, and we cannot guarantee that a site's future contents will continue to meet our high standards of quality and educational value. Be advised that children should be closely supervised whenever they access the Internet.

INDEX